Walking the Arroyo

Poems

Debbi Brody

Cyberwit.net
HIG 45 Kaushambi Kunj, Kalindipuram
Allahabad - 211011 (U.P.) India
http://www.cyberwit.net
Tel: +(91) 9415091004 +(91) (532) 2552257
E-mail: info@cyberwit.net

Printed at Repro India Limited.

NATURE HAIKU-ARROYO

August Cactus plums
Due in October, early
Food for a harsh Fall.

In one square yard
I spy nine varieties
Of yellow wild flowers.

Bees prefer purple
Alfalfa over pink
Cinquefoil

Cold nights, cool mornings,
Sunshine warm days, perfect
Dog walking weather

Thirty-two degrees,
Leaves on the locust trees
Crackle.

Cooper's hawk flies
Over dog in frozen canyon,
Small mouse in claw

Egg daddy dashes in
Assists momma raven chase
Away thief kestrel

Searching for tanagers
Singing in trees,
I find two mockingbirds.

Given enough rain,
It turns out dandelions
Can grow in sand.

Animal tracks in
Thin mud. Snake's wiggle path, makes
The ants' smooth runway

Chamisa sweetened
Air, hummingbird clicks, angel
Wing clouds sweep sky.

Autumn or fall
To your feet beauty in green
Purple and yellow.

Fairies surely dwell
In these delicate
Magic-fluff flowers.

NATURE

An Ecstasy of Wild Flowers

My heart can hardly hold
The blue red purple orange pink white yellow
Fields of flowers
In this typically barely blooming
Nearly barren land.

Walking in this underbrush,
I'm Emily Carr, painting
Green pines with watercolor –
Calling them forth to life.

Paw at pack rats' den
Sniff rock squirrels' hole
Chase, don't catch jack rabbit
Perfect dog day afternoon.

Spring; Santa Fe

Listen to bees
Sip fruit flowers on trees,
Birds imbibe, drunk on pink petals.
Tuesday expect snow.

Kids play in the arroyo,
Dig up rocky treasures,
As dark sky moves
Towards them.

Basia reads about a rabbit
Wrapped in a fast food napkin,
Human ritual for a wild thing.

Our town so small
I know the where and when
Of this small dead.

Pack rats love city engineers
Who build impenetrable
Rock houses held together
By chain link keeping
Out ravens and owls.

THOUGHT HAIKU

Sooner than was guessed
New Mexico will be sea
Side prime property.

No matter the number
Of clock checks,
I arrive home when I do.

I don't mind being
His pain killer, I do things
For our love.

Lava, like you,
Beautiful dangerous.

Mother's Day getting you down?
Hit the trails,
Where bouquets abound.

My dog and I
At last the same age,
Same arthritis.

THOUGHT

Snow melt exposes
Needles and (not as colorful
As last year's) condoms.

Cigarette butts and alcohol
Minis burst forth
As innocent cousins.

Trust

Married at twenty,
I didn't settle in
Until sixty. Yes, it took
Twice my prior life time
To trust, to believe
We will always be together.

That changes everything.

The women are always small enough
to jump up and wrap their legs around
the muscular man as he carries her up
the stairs to the bedroom where they rip
off their clothes before falling into bed
and having their best ever orgasms.

My unending network of pals are called books,
But my best buddy is "language",
The word itself sounds like stretching out
On an antique chase lounge.

It turns out
The ordinary
As profound as the extraordinary,
Each detail
A miracle of life.

Miracle

This morning when I ask
A befuddled girl twisting
Her head back and forth
In the middle of the arroyo,
If she's ok, she says yes,
I'm fine, just waiting for
my boyfriend, thanks for asking.

In 25 years of walking this before-work path,
I have spoken to dozens of young women
And girls, often homeless, always hungry,
Some abused by boyfriends or parents,
Some lost, separated
From the high school track group,
Or dropped off at the wrong street,
All of whom burst into tears
And even soul wracking sobs
When offered the small kindness of inquiry.

This morning's Cinderella,
As I have grown to call them
Over the years, is fine, just fine.
Her clear eyes prove it.

Walking home on Camino Carlos Rey,
I try to explain to my dog
Why diesel makes her sneeze.
Large particulate I say.
She says, Check out the titmouse
And this wonderful smelling poop.

Chronic ptsd- ers

Functional due to unconditional love from a dog,
The only mammal that ever rejoiced
In their company with no thought
Of manipulation or personal gain,
Chose tents in the arroyo's
Underbrush rather than part
With their lifeline.

www.ingramcontent.com/pod-product-compliance
Lightning Source LLC
Chambersburg PA
CBHW051830130726
47987CB00003B/1477